SMALL HOMES

short on space, big on style

TERRA

THE AUTHORS

As the founder of Taverne Agency, **Nathalie Taverne** has spent the past eleven years working with the world's finest interior, lifestyle and food photographers, ensuring their work appears in the world's finest magazines. Within the Taverne collection, original and inspirational homes from around the world are brought together under one roof, with the stories of those who design and live in them as fascinating as the photographs are beautiful. Nathalie and her husband and business partner Robert Borghuis live and work in Amsterdam and together find time to raise their two children, Elena and John.

Having begun her writing career on the *Financial Times'* award-winning *How To Spend It* magazine, **Anna Lambert** went on to spend three years working in the Netherlands, where she began her collaboration with Nathalie Taverne. Anna's work has appeared in interiors magazines worldwide, including *Australian Vogue Living*, *World of Interiors*, *Elle Decoration* and *Elle Wonen*, and she is the author of *Easy Living* and *Inspirational Apartments*, both published by Terra Lannoo. She lives with her husband and two daughters in the UK.

© 2010 Uitgeverij Terra Lannoo B.V.
P.O.Box 614, 6800 AP Arnhem
The Netherlands
info@terralannoo.nl
www.terralannoo.nl
Uitgeverij Terra is part of the Lannoo group, Belgium

TEXT AND IMAGES: © 2010 Taverne Agency B.V.
Lisdoddelaan 79
1087 KB Amsterdam
The Netherlands
www.taverneagency.com

COMPILATION: Nathalie Taverne
TEXT: Anna Lambert
DESIGN: Manon Jansen for Pier 3 Creatie, Lelystad
PRINTED AND BOUND: Leo Paper Products Ltd., Hong Kong

ISBN 978 90 8989 205 8
NUR 454
Also published in Dutch as Maximaal Wonen
(ISBN 978 90 8989 191 4)

CITY COLOUR 06

Lifting the look 07
Where lime adds zest 12
The hard-working home 16
Finding inspiration 22
All that glisters 28

CITY NEUTRAL 34

A whiter shade of pale 35
The only way is up 40
Making big-hearted pieces work 46
Who says it's size that counts? 52

COUNTRY COLOUR 58

The warmest of welcomes 59
Sugared-almond colours 66
A work of art 72

COUNTRY NEUTRAL 78

Creating a place for everything 79
Using simple, natural elements 84
Flamboyant, feminine and full of charm 88

Credits & contacts 96

SMALL HOMES THRIVE

If you've picked up this book, the chances are it's because you live in a small home yourself and are looking for inspiration. But let's begin with a bit of reassurance – because, in a world where phrases such as 'big is better' and 'size matters' are frequently bandied about, it's easy to think that small homes are in some way inferior to their capacious cousins. Not so! In fact, while we're talking in clichés, the space-constrained home-owner's motto should surely be 'small is beautiful'. The advantages of living in a smaller space are many: for a start, those who live in them are forced to be more disciplined in what they acquire and display – and what they recycle, give to charity or send to the skip. We small-home owners (and I'm speaking from personal experience here) must find ingenious solutions to the perennial storage challenge, and ask of every piece of furniture that we add to our rooms 'will it earn its keep?' and – ideally – 'can it serve more than one purpose?' If the answer is 'yes', small low tables find themselves reinvented as stools; square, hollow stools find themselves reinvented as storage boxes and tables find themselves doubling up as both eating areas and work stations. Shelves can be added to almost any nook or cranny, while alcoves and even cupboards can be transformed into mini-offices and studies – the list of options is limited only by your imagination. From sticking to one shade of colour in every room to strategic placing of furniture, mirrors and pictures, there's a whole host of tricks that you can employ to maximise the sense of space within your home – ideas that we'll be exploring in the pages to come. In many of the homes we'll be looking at, though, there's no desire to 'make things look bigger'. Instead these are houses and apartments that positively celebrate their lack of size, delighting in the 'cabinet of curiosities'-type quirkiness that is so often the hallmark of the smaller home and that lends them so much charm. With their all-embracing proportions, small spaces have a real advantage when it comes to creating true sanctuaries – intimate spaces in which their owners can relax, work, entertain or just recharge their batteries. So read on and remember: not only can little spaces be transformed into the loveliest of homes; on a practical level, they'll always take less time to redecorate, de-clutter and tidy than their larger counterparts. Sometimes the best things really do come in small packages.

UNDER IMAGINATIVE OWNERSHIP

The clean lines of contemporary city homes mean even the most bijoux spaces can benefit from a splash of colour.

CITY COLOUR

LIFTING THE LOOK

In urban homes where space is limited, make colour work by combining a disciplined approach with a sense of playfulness.

So often, those of us who live in smaller homes are told there's a list of decorative rules we've got to stick to: don't overcrowd spaces, keep colours pale and uniform throughout the various rooms or zones – play safe, basically. But one of the joys of the smaller home is the opportunity it offers for small-scale experimentation. This London flat is a great example of how it's possible to break rules yet still achieve a coherent, beautiful look. At first glance, it all appears pretty orthodox: the walls and sofa are white, bookshelves extend right up to the ceiling thus lifting the eye upward and increasing the sense of space, a mirrored console allows light to bounce around making the room appear bigger – so far, then, so conformist. Throw an antique Biedermeier dining table, classic 20th-century chairs, patterned wallpaper, graphic rugs and ornate lamps into the mix, though, and things start to get really interesting. So how has the owner ensured her disparate pieces don't make this small space appear muddled and over-crowded? For a start, while she's boldly plumped for colour, she's limited her use of it to a couple of accent shades. The apartment's key colours of feminine pink, red and turquoise are contained in the living room rug and are also picked up elsewhere. Warmer shades of red are used in the bedroom, for instance, while use of the predominant secondary colour, deep turquoise, is restricted to accessories so it doesn't overwhelm the smaller space.

Limiting accent colours to a few shades – here pink, red and turquoise – adds interest to contemporary-classic small homes without overwhelming them.

Choose your colours and stick to them and you can't go far wrong.

Choice of furniture is important, too. In smaller homes, it can be wise to select pieces that will merge into the background – as the sofa next to the white wall does in this home, for instance. Alternatively, choose 'invisible' furniture – witness the Perspex coffee table and shelves and the classic Bertoia diamond chair, both in the living room. What appears to be a lack of solidity in their design ensures that, visually, they don't block the line of vision, which again helps to maximise the sense of space.

Where there's less room for furniture or if you're decorating on a strict budget, a good rule is to buy less and buy better. Here, what little the owner has is undeniably worth having: Dorothee Becker's Uten Silo wall-mounted plastic storage for

Vitra, chairs by Charles and Ray Eames and Arne Jacobsen, and an unusual oil-can table in the bedroom from interior designer Andrew Martin.

Finally, it's an element of surprise that will always personalise a home. You might not expect to find wallpaper used in a kitchen but in this home Manuel Canovas' glamorous design, printed in black and white, is sufficiently unfussy to work in this pared-down space.

WHERE LIME ADDS ZEST

If by any chance you're looking at the picture, right, and thinking 'but this room looks big to me', bear in mind that that's what's so impressive about this New York space: it's all a cleverly-constructed illusion...

There's no denying that the proportions of the room shown here are lofty and it's enviably light-filled. But all we're talking about is one large living area, a bedroom and bathroom and – as you'll see overleaf – a tiny kitchen. Here the owners have employed canny tricks to ensure the apartment looks larger than it actually is. The surprise element comes via juxtaposition: the Imac that sits atop the inlaid walnut Carlton desk and the Gustavian-style sofa and chairs, all upholstered – and updated – in zingy lime and turquoise fabrics that are reproductions of designs from the 1950s. Playing a key part in linking the various elements is a luxurious cream rug, which connects the two open-plan halves of the living space and anchors what might otherwise have appeared as disparate pieces of furniture.

In the kitchen, there's a great example of the sort of cosiness only small spaces can offer. By adding the banquettes to an alcove, the owners have created a little nook in which they're as happy to spend time reading and relaxing as they are eating – and the wall-mounted magazine rack (similar examples are available worldwide from stores such as IKEA) means reading materials are kept out of the way but close at hand. Meanwhile, by introducing the same turquoise and blue shades as used elsewhere in the apartment, a sense of continuity and spaciousness is conveyed.

Colour provides
UNITY AND STYLE

Colour is used here to give the various rooms a space-enhancing sense of unity and a common stylistic 'theme'– one that's emphasised through choice of furniture, accessories, fabrics and art.

THE HARD-WORKING HOME

In small homes, it's imperative that every piece of furniture functions truly effectively – and has a dual purpose if possible.

This Copenhagen home really is small – the owner has just 44m² to play with. She's kept it looking spacious firstly by cutting clutter to the absolute minimum and secondly by opting for multi-functional furnishings such as, in the living room, stools that can alternatively serve as tables. Elsewhere, neon lights provide illumination, a shot of colour, and serve as artistic pieces in their own right. In the owner's bedroom, space under the bed could be used for storage – with a valence to hide it if desired. By using the same colour on both the wooden floor and the cupboard doors, the eye is drawn upwards creating a greater sense of space. Using one colour on walls, doors, ceilings and floor is a great way to create the illusion of space, so consider doing this in your own home if at all possible. In the kitchen, meanwhile, walls are utilised for storage, with boxes turned on their sides and used as simple shelving.

Above all it's quirky wall-mounted art-works, plus textiles in the form of decorative cushions, functional tea-towels and vibrant pot-holders, that add interest to this home, giving the owner the best of both worlds: a sense of space and a truly individual home.

No matter how much – or how little – space you've got, there's always room to add interest and detail in unexpected places.

Here, pictures, installation art and even lettering enliven walls and furniture.

only love give it away it's o

PX 43 044

FINDING INSPIRATION

Discipline and restraint are the watchwords in creating a successful small home. It's not necessarily about limiting your possessions but, rather, about keeping everything unfussy and unified in style.

The owner of this New York apartment has clearly found her passion: south Asian antiques. Because she's kept the background colours in her home neutral, though, she's able to indulge it without overwhelming the small space. Low-level seating in the form of pouffes and cushions creates an illusion of space – and it's pretty easy to make the sort of settee-style sofa shown overleaf using inexpensively-bought rectangular foam cushions upholstered in cotton or linen slipcovers. The art in this home carries on the relaxed, informal feel. Frames, of course, take up wall space so paintings are displayed on the floor, which is the level at which guests are encouraged to sit. Keeping artworks unframed or the walls clear are

other ways of making rooms feel bigger. Lighting is of course key in any home but, especially in smaller spaces, it can be a great way to emphasise proportion and create a sense of drama in nooks, crannies and corners. In the dining room here, the simple light fitting in the centre of the ceiling looks like a 'drop in the ocean' – choosing a small fitting has made the space look larger than it actually is.

Window treatments are another aspect to consider carefully in the small-space home and this one's a great example of the advantages of keeping things as unfussy as possible. Here, simple louvred blinds provide privacy while also allowing the light to filter beautifully into each room, yet they don't take up unnecessary space

Bringing the outside in
AND THE INSIDE OUT

Carrying the pink of the textiles from the dining area outside ensures the space flows and creates maximum impact. Elsewhere, the owner makes the most of wall-hung storage.

Being able to see space under the sofa creates the illusion of roominess,
while shutters allow light to filter into the room yet still leave valuable wall space free.

around the window. Elsewhere, in the dining area for instance, windows are left completely bare. It's worth taking stock of any spaces in your own home to identify areas that you could be using for storage. In this kitchen, for instance, rather than the traditional splash-back behind the cooker, the owner has added shelves so that everything she needs is close to hand yet out of the way. It's another example of the importance of a disciplined eye: if you go for the open-shelving option, it's always going to look more attractive if you've restricted your choice of homeware to pieces that not only function well but that also look pretty on display – and that's exactly what the owner has done here.

If you're looking for a starting point to inspire your home decor, a picture or piece of pottery that you love or the colours or style of a fabric that appeals to you should all prompt plenty of ideas – and you could create your own 'mood board' of things that you like, which you can refer to throughout the decorating process.

ALL THAT GLISTERS

Plenty of light will always help a small home look bigger but it doesn't have to come via lamps or mirrors; here, it's art that provides the illumination.

As the 1940s' classic song goes, 'you've got to accentuate the positive, eliminate the negative' and that's just what the owner of this apartment is doing. While horizontal space is at a premium in her Melbourne home, there's plenty of room overhead and she's drawn attention to this in the room shown opposite by her choice of a graphic black and white blind, rectangular cupboard doors, an angular chair and the photo frame that sits on top of the mantelshelf. All these verticals help to lead the eye upward, so it's the high ceilings you notice rather than the less-than-generous proportions of the rooms. Elsewhere, glittering artworks bring a luminous glow, with distressed paint finishes on the walls adding to the sense of a home that's shimmering, almost ethereal. Paint washes can work particularly well in smaller homes, allowing experimentation with strong colour while at the same time avoiding that too-dense, heavy look that might otherwise be created. Where strong colour is used in a solid block – on the orange wall, for instance – it's only in moderation. In other places, vibrant colour is diluted by plenty of white or used as a hazy paint wash. The custodian of this home is all too aware of colour's impact on mood – that's why stimulating orange is used in her work area and restful mauve in her dressing room, with appetite-enhancing red decorating the dining space. Toning everything down is the wood that's used within this home, from the distressed finish of the floor and the doors to the more formal, white-washed lines of tongue-and-groove wall cladding and rectangular panelling.

In rooms where there's little space for furniture, stick to the basics. Then create an impact with one single, show-stopping piece,

such as the chandelier in the bedroom below.

Colour works so well in this home because either it's used to pack a punch over a small area

or, in larger ones, it's diluted both with plenty of white and by using it as a hazy paint wash.

Not only sight but other senses are soothed in this home, too: scented candles burn, gentle music plays. It sounds obvious but all too often, in the rush to create homes that look good, we forget about the other elements so essential to the creation of a true sanctuary for ourselves. Surrounding yourself with things that you love to look at is only part of the story – whatever size your home, there is always room for delicious fragrances and a small sound system that enables you to listen to your favourite music. There's an old rule: any space filled with flowers, books and music will always feel welcoming. Fortunately, these are three things that almost any budget – and any amount of space – can be stretched to accommodate.

Keeping to a colour palette of white, black, browns and
greys creates a calm yet sophisticated vibe.

CITY
NEUTRAL

A WHITER SHADE OF PALE

When teamed with natural-style accessories, this home's palette of whites, creams and browns succeeds in accentuating a sense of light and space.

This Amsterdam apartment's living room is a great example of what can be achieved when a disciplined owner chooses one colour and sticks to it. Here, white walls, ceiling and floor create a seamless, airy look – and it's the restful atmosphere that seems the most important thing about this home. An all-white palette runs the risk of looking overly-clinical and cold but the owner has avoided this by selecting earthy, natural accessories in warmer shades of brown: the rug, cushions and the little wicker stool. Even the simple arrangement of bare twigs continues the natural theme, while the generous scale of the arrangement helps create an illusion of space. With storage at a premium, the owner has cleverly selected a bench that functions as a home for books and magazines as well as a seating option.

Off the kitchen, the little dining nook is given a warmer feel by the addition of taupe table linen and wooden furniture, while a wall lamp provides accent lighting. There's room in almost any home, whatever its size, for such areas: they can be 'carved out' of existing spaces and separated from the rest of the room by creating a different atmosphere within them. Here, for instance, the wall lamp is the sort you would find in a larger dining room or study, even though it's used within a utilitarian kitchen, so it helps create an entirely different mood within the room.

Continuity is key to this home's
SPACIOUS, RESTFUL FEEL

On the balcony, too, soft colours and wicker furniture are the order of the day.

THE ONLY WAY IS UP

Sometimes making a small house work as a pleasing and practical home is all about thinking 'outside the box' – in this case, literally.

When a young Melbourne-based architect couple acquired what was then a tiny terraced house, they wanted to create the illusion of more space. Although the site they inherited measures barely 3.8 by 25 metres, the home they've created feels – impressively – much larger than it actually is. This is because they've accentuated the verticals wherever possible, adding an open central staircase that doubles as a light-well and thus floods their home with sunshine. While the living room may be miniscule, what you notice is its extraordinarily high ceiling (five metres), which is further accentuated by floor-to-ceiling bookshelves. Elsewhere the ceiling drops to a more standard height, a factor that creates unexpected levels and adds interest throughout the house. Meanwhile, in the open kitchen and informal living and dining area, a vast sky-light ensures lots of natural light and prevents the space seeming overly 'boxy'. More light enters the space thanks to the floor-to-ceiling glass doors, which can be pulled right back allowing the timber deck and rear courtyard garden to link seamlessly with the interior of the house.

A simple colour palette is teamed with exposed girders, modern art and textured paint and plaster finishes to create a home that's coolly contemporary, yet full of light and warmth.

Simple materials such as
CONCRETE, WOOD AND STAINLESS STEEL

help give this home its airy, minimalistic feel, while splashes of colour and a pared-down
art collection ensure it feels lived in and loved.

MAKING BIG-HEARTED PIECES WORK

Old and new, classic and cutting edge can sit easily aside one another when selected with a sure hand.

Having looked at the photos of this pretty and generously-proportioned Copenhagen apartment you might be surprised to learn that, in fact, its owner has only 75m² to play with. So what tricks has she employed to make it appear larger? Undeniably the high ceilings help, but it's also about a well-edited mix of furnishings, pattern and colour. Contrast is what counts here – the contrast between a classic chesterfield sofa and a 20th-century Jacobsen chair or between the 'fussiness' of a fine wool rug from Pakistan and simple lights from IKEA. Practicality is vital to this home too – hence, in the living room, a table that may double up as both a work space and a dining area has been chosen for its sturdy versatility.

Anchoring the entire single-floor home is the unpolished wooden floor, with the wood adding interest through its faded grain. Pattern is introduced via floor rugs which are positioned vertically to allow a narrow room to seem wider. These beautiful pieces are placed side by side to create the appearance of a whole, and it's worth remembering that a generous rug will always help a smaller space appear larger. In other words, use mats for bathrooms or foot-wiping only.

Older pieces of furniture, too, are a good way to add interest to smaller rooms, particularly period homes. The Arne Jacobsen Swan chair shown here, for instance, is that bit more special simply because it's slightly battered – obviously

A mix of old and new gives this space a timeless style, while a vivid slash of red adds an element of surprise.

A couple of rugs anchor pieces within the room.

it's been well-loved for many years. If at all possible, choose furniture with bases that sit slightly off the floor – if you can see empty space beneath chairs and sofas it increases the impression of overall spaciousness. In the kitchen of this apartment, the owner has done a great job of fully exploiting the space at her disposal. The high window allows plenty of light into the room, so she's had no qualms about placing a shelf across its top section to create more storage space. Filling it with pretty glassware means the light can still filter in easily. Open cupboards and hanging ceramic lights also give the room character. A corner of the room is given over to dining, where the feel is charmingly old-fashioned, with a wall-clock and lace-curtain adding to the atmosphere. All in all, this apartment shows that a passion for classic furnishings – and plenty of them – can be indulged within a smaller space without any need for compromise.

WHO SAYS IT'S SIZE THAT COUNTS?

This home proves that, with ingenuity, a willingness to de-clutter and a flair for colour, smaller homes can be every bit as gorgeous as their larger relations...

Part of a building dating from 1908, this Californian apartment should provide inspiration for anyone who's downsizing. Its owner moved here from a large three-bedroom period home. This one, though far smaller, enjoys a wooded location in the city suburbs and, despite being carved out of a larger house, still retains its own entrance. Moreover it has bags of charm and, as its owner says, 'the space felt good'. Having to pare down her possessions to fit into her new home has undoubtedly honed the owner's prioritisation skills and she's reduced her things down to what she considers to be important, precious and necessary. "It frees up my mind for more creative thinking," she says – something that's important given that she both lives and works at home. She's certainly come up with plenty of creative solutions to deal with the lack of space, such as choosing a contemporary streamlined leather sofa for her living room, customising a cupboard with special shelves, thereby turning it into a little office space for herself, and creating a dining area within a small alcove. A bedroom, meanwhile, is transformed into a manageable space by adding much-needed storage above the headboard. Elsewhere, castors have been added to an old kitchen table so that it can be rolled out and used as a work surface or pushed against the wall when more floor space is needed. The owner's also got a real flair for giving

No one could call this home understated or short of possessions, but it's a characterful as opposed to an overwhelming look that works so well

because the owner seems to have found or created a place for everything.

old things a contemporary purpose: in the bathroom, for instance, industrial clipboards are used to display the delicate vintage textiles she collects. Rather than being discarded, twigs collected on walks in the woods are displayed like low-key living sculptures.

Colour is used in this home in a particularly lively way: each open shelf in the kitchen, for instance, is enlivened by a different shade – neutral splashes of earthy brown, rust, or teal blue. In the bedroom and living room, white wooden panelling ensures that the strong mustard colour used both on the walls and the ceiling doesn't become overpowering.

When used in rustic spaces, colour adds playfulness and informality, creating homes that are bursting with energy and charm.

COUNTRY COLOUR

THE WARMEST OF WELCOMES

The stony, rough-and-ready facade of this Italian home belies its cosy, practical interior.

This little Tuscan house dates from the late 17th century and has been lovingly brought back to life by an Italian-Danish couple. Wherever possible they've reused original materials, keeping the historical spirit of the place intact. The stone flooring that runs throughout the house is the ideal choice for this sort of home – cool in summer, heat-absorbing in winter. Modern additions include the new staircase, which incorporates some of the house's original stones. The fireplace here is a key feature of their home and a fire stays lit throughout the winter. The kitchen, meanwhile, mixes old with new: tiles here date from the 19th century and originally came from Naples, while the granite sink is another old piece. By contrast, chairs around the old Tuscan dining table include Hans Wegner's classic Wishbone design. The sparkle of glass comes courtesy of the couple's chandelier collection.

One of the designer-owner's favourite spaces is her 'bolthole' – a room containing all sorts of bits and pieces, ranging from religious paraphernalia to buttons, books and ribbons – where she can experiment and develop ideas to her heart's content. Another special space is the bedroom, which features a colourful eiderdown by the designer Lisa Corti and an antique Turkish rug. The man of the house devised the coat-hanger system that hangs from the ceiling here, allowing him to display various items from his wardrobe as decorations.

Wherever possible, the owners of this Tuscan cottage have used authentic materials and finishes: timbered ceilings, plastered walls and exposed stone work.

The result is a home with both a heart and a sense of its history.

In the living room, a favourite piece is an unusual battered chesterfield, upholstered in petrol-blue leather, which the couple rescued from a local spa. Nearby hang modern artworks from Denmark.

This is the sort of small house in which people are so busy living life that they are not overly concerned with making their space 'work harder' or seem larger than it actually is. Their relaxed approach makes for a home that revels in its lack of constraints and its wealth of different treasures – testament to its owners' various adventures, their careers and the influences of their different homelands. It's worth remembering, then, that sometimes there's little point in attempting to maximise space within a smaller home – instead, it's as simple as filling the space you have with things and people that you love, then enjoying it to the max.

SUGARED-ALMOND COLOURS

Decorated in easy-breezy pastel shades, this Danish seaside cottage is a bijoux space that's ideal for relaxing breaks and family getaways.

This little house works so well because it's got such a firm sense of its own identity. Wooden tongue and grooving throughout immediately proclaim it a rustic space, while white-washed timbers and a high, open ceiling add to the feel. Though it's a colourful place, the variety of shades used all come from the pastel end of the spectrum, so mint green sits comfortably next to baby blue and the owner's favourite colour, lilac. Moreover, the colour is used not just on walls and furnishings but it's also picked up in accessories such as the lilac tablecloth and the pale green milk-glass cups and saucers. Above all, though, colour works here because it's diluted with liberal amounts of white, and when white flooring extends up into white walls and ceiling, a sense of light and space will always be the result. Similarly, upstairs in the children's bedroom – complete with space-saving bunk bed – the room looks larger because the green of the floor is echoed throughout the room.

The kick-off-your-shoes-and-relax vibe is accentuated through the shabby-chic choice of furniture. Nothing here is too precious to be jumped on, a consideration that's so important when you're talking about homes for young children, as is the case here. Slipcovers mean everything can be thrown into the washing machine as and when necessary, while walls and floors can easily be wiped down. This really is the ideal easy-living home – one that demonstrates that sometimes spaciousness is a state of mind.

Home, Sweet Home
IN SHERBERT-SWEETIE COLOURS

The palette used for this house is sufficiently soft and fresh to ensure the effect is romantic
and feminine – never overwhelmingly twee.

A WORK OF ART

This pretty house – both a living space and a potter's studio – proves that colour works anywhere and in any climate to enliven and invigorate the home.

Given the vibrant, sunny atmosphere of this little house, you might assume it's located somewhere that enjoys balmy weather – such as Spain, or maybe Italy. Perhaps surprisingly, it's on the Danish island of Zealand and the fact that the colours shown here look so cosy proves that even cooler shades, when used cleverly, can give off a warmth of their own no matter what the climate.

The ceramicist-owner of this cottage clearly loves green and has used virtually every shade of it within her home, from arsenic to mint to pistachio. By mixing it with warmer colours, such as the red-brown of the woodwork on the kitchen cupboards, it takes on a heat of its own that even the cool northern light can't diminish. In fact cooler colours can work well in smaller homes, simply because the cosy nature of small-scale living immediately stops them from seeming overly clinical. It helps, too, that this house is enlivened with an eclectic and fascinating mix of objects – the kitchen tiles (made by the owner) and the floral eiderdown on the sofa in the living room, for instance. In the bedroom, the beds – with their rounded shape and gold finish – bring a curvaceous richness to the room, creating a comfortable, welcoming feel here, too.

A simple colour palette works really well in country homes, allowing their natural setting, rather than any internal decoration, to dominate.

COUNTRY NEUTRAL

CREATING A PLACE FOR EVERYTHING

Ingenuity is a useful skill to have when turning a small space into a home – and that's something the owners of this house undoubtedly possess.

This house in the French countryside is a terrific example of how to make the most of the sort of awkward nooks and crannies that are often found in smaller homes. Yes, they add bags of charm, but when you're short of space their angles can prove hard to work around, especially when it comes to fitting in storage space. Here, the owners have managed to do just that, however, with bookshelves above doorways and beds, cooking utensils hung on hooks and bespoke shelving built into eaves. There may not be many rooms in this home but – this being a converted barn – they all boast impressively high ceilings and the owners have exploited this to the full. A row of pegs halfway up a wall, for instance, not only proves useful

for displaying a collection of hats, it also succeeds in visually 'lowering' the ceiling, helping to create a more intimate feel within the otherwise cavernous space.

The neutral colour scheme of natural greys, blues and browns is reflected in simple ticking-fabric bed linen and textiles, old French crockery, enamelled lampshades and black-and-white photo portraits on the walls. This palette not only complements the surrounding countryside but also has the sort of pared-down feel that's ideal for a relaxed country retreat.

Making the most
OF WHAT YOU'VE GOT

There's no denying this is a gorgeous home but its awkward corners could have made it difficult to live in.
By adding bespoke shelves, pegs and hooks the owners have cleverly solved any storage and display problems.

USING SIMPLE, NATURAL ELEMENTS

Materials in the smaller home don't have to be sophisticated. Here, the owners have used wood and stone to create their ideal space.

Single-storey houses aren't common in Italy but that's what we're looking at here. Interestingly, the house belongs to a group of guys and the interior designers have reflected their masculine, low-key tastes. What's really striking, though, is the atmosphere that's created in a home where less really is more. The place isn't cluttered – instead, the designers have concentrated on creating a few striking images: retaining the original granite flooring throughout, the specially-made wooden fire-surround, the chair carved from one single hunk of wood and, of course, the lights. Danish designer Cecille Manz's black Caravaggio ceiling lamps, complete with their red cords, serve as a reminder that, while on a practical level light is vital in any home, it should serve as a decorative element too. With so many different styles of shades currently on the market, there's no excuse for sticking to the banal or second rate.

As ever it's a question of adding interest to a home via contrast and, here, a chandelier and the odd flash of bright red furniture or a highly decorative rug keep the overall feel of the home on the right side of Spartan. The result is a living space that's functional and fun, yet restful too.

Coolly contemporary living
BUT WITH PLENTY TO CATCH THE EYE

This space manages to combine practicality with engaging detail in the form of funky lighting, the odd piece of colourful furniture and a gloriously patterned rug.

FLAMBOYANT, FEMININE AND FULL OF CHARM

All the world's a stage in this glorious home – so take inspiration from a make-believe world where glamour's the order of the day.

The opposite to the 'less is more' approach is, of course, 'if you've got it, flaunt it'. What makes this Johannesburg-suburbs home particularly intriguing is the way in which an effusive, opulent style has been made to work within a very small space. Certainly, one of the things that helps is the owner's confidence – she loves what's she's got and she's keen to celebrate it. Having spent time studying in Paris, her collage of memorabilia collected from the city is given pride of place within the hall. Though it serves primarily to remind her of a fantastic experience abroad, it's also a great example of a Mood Board, where images, colours and fabrics are brought together as inspiration for a design process. These are particularly useful when it comes to planning home decoration.

Though the style of this home is unashamedly feminine, it's worth noting that a couple live here. The woman of the house has toned down her look by adding 'grown up' and less-girly touches such as the black walls in the bedroom, the specimen-like treasures displayed under glass domes and quirky pieces of modern art. Outside, too, the feel is restrained: simple garden furniture and a lemon tree – a perfect spot in which to enjoy the warmth of the sun.

There are plenty of tips the small-home owner can glean from this space – stencilling is an inexpensive alternative to wallpaper, allowing you to experiment

Smaller outdoor spaces, of course, also benefit from thoughtful planning. Here, a shady corner has been transformed into a relaxing spot.

White furnishings create a cool, clean and simple vibe.

with pattern and scale and it can easily be painted over if you don't like the final effect. Take inspiration, too, from the owner's display techniques: pieces under glass and on plinths, or presented almost as if they're items dressing the set of a play. Such theatricality, if implemented with brio, can work well in smaller homes – look how a presumably formerly lack-lustre sofa has been given a new lease of life just by the simple act of draping it with a lavish piece of silk. This style doesn't appeal to everyone, but if you can see yourself living in a home like this, it's a fantastic way of creating a wholly unique and personal world within your own four walls.

CREDITS:

COVER IMAGE FRONT
Photographer Earl Carter - Producer Anne Marie Kiely

COVER IMAGE BACK
Photographer Karina Tengberg - Producer Tami Christiansen

CITY COLOUR
P 7, 8, 11
Photographer Lisa Cohen - Producer Vanessa Barnaby
P 13, 14, 15
Photographer and producer Ngoc Minh Ngo
P 17, 18, 19, 20, 21
Photographer Karina Tengberg - Producer Tami Christiansen
P 23, 24, 25, 26
Photographer and producer Ngoc Minh Ngo
P 29, 30, 31, 33
Photographer Earl Carter - Producer Anne Marie Kiely

CITY NEUTRAL
P 35, 37, 38, 39
Photographer Marjon Hoogervorst - Producer Annemarie Reinders
P 40, 42, 43, 44, 45
Photographer Mikkel Vang - Producer Helen Redmond
P 47, 48, 49, 50
Photographer Mikkel Vang - Producer Christine Rudolph
P 52, 54, 55, 56
Photographer and producer Ngoc Minh Ngo

COUNTRY COLOUR
P 59, 60, 62, 63, 65
Photographer Ditte Isager - Producer Christine Rudolph
P 67, 68, 69, 70, 71
Photographer Nathalie Krag - Producer Anja Alfieri
P 72, 73, 74, 75, 76
Photographer Nathalie Krag

COUNTRY NEUTRAL
P 79, 81, 82, 83
Photographer and producer Ngoc Minh Ngo
P 84, 86, 87
Photographer Ditte Isager - Producer Christine Rudolph
P 89, 90, 91, 93, 94, 95
Photographer Alexander van Berge - Producer Genneth Lyn

CONTACTS:

CITY COLOUR
P 12, 13, 14, 15
chaircouture.com
P 16, 17, 18, 19, 20, 21
www.byfribert.dk
P 22, 23, 24, 25, 26
www.layla-bklyn.com
P 28, 29, 30, 31, 32, 33
www.suttongallery.com.au

CITY NEUTRAL
P 40, 41, 42, 43, 44, 45
www.oconnorandhoule.com
P 52, 53, 54, 55, 56, 57
www.sherryolsen.net

COUNTRY COLOUR
P 58, 59, 60, 61, 62, 63, 64, 65
www.andreabrugi.com
P 66, 67, 68, 69, 70, 71
www.cremedelacremealaedgar.dk
P 72, 73, 74, 75, 76, 77
www.arendal-ceramics.com

COUNTRY NEUTRAL
P 79, 80, 81, 82, 83
www.danieljasiak.com
P 84, 85, 86, 87
www.andreabrugi.com
P 88, 89, 90, 91, 92, 93, 94, 95
www.leelynch.co.za

All photographers are represented by Taverne Agency.
More of their work can be found on www.taverneagency.com